Financial Planner

2017 | Pi Luna Press

ISBN: 978-0998686066

Pi Luna Press
Santa Fe, New Mexico
www.pilunapress.com

How To Use This Book

Monthly Budget

At the beginning of every month, you can create your monthly budget. Enter your projected amounts at the beginning of the month, and then enter your actual amounts at the end of the month to see how well you stuck to your budget.

Budget	Projected	Actual

Daily Schedule

You can write down you appointments and daily activities in the schedule section.

Sunday	Monday	Tuesday	Wednesday

To Do List

Each week has a to do list to help you manage your time and be more productive.

Thursday	Friday	Saturday	To Do List
			☐
			☐

Financial Transactions

At the bottom of each day, you can record your transactions to help you track your spending. Use these amounts to help you make your budget each month.

Transactions		Transactions		Transactions		Transactions	
Category	Amount	Category	Amount	Category	Amount	Category	Amount
	$		$		$		$
	$		$		$		$

January

January's Budget

Income	Projected	Actual
Total Income		

Savings & Investments	Projected	Actual
Total Savings & Investments		

Expenses	Projected	Actual
Total Expenses		

Ending Balance	Projected	Actual
Total Income - Total Savings & Investments - Total Expenses =		

January 1 - 7

1 Sunday	2 Monday	3 Tuesday	4 Wednesday
7am			
8am			
9am			
10am			
11am			
12pm			
1pm			
2pm			
3pm			
4pm			
5pm			
6pm			
7pm			

Transactions

Category	Amount
	$
	$
	$
	$
	$

Transactions

Category	Amount
	$
	$
	$
	$
	$

Transactions

Category	Amount
	$
	$
	$
	$
	$

Transactions

Category	Amount
	$
	$
	$
	$
	$

5 Thursday

6 Friday

7 Saturday

To Do List

- [ ]
- [ ]
- [ ]
- [ ]
- [ ]
- [ ]
- [ ]
- [ ]
- [ ]
- [ ]
- [ ]
- [ ]
- [ ]
- [ ]
- [ ]
- [ ]
- [ ]
- [ ]
- [ ]
- [ ]
- [ ]
- [ ]
- [ ]
- [ ]
- [ ]
- [ ]
- [ ]
- [ ]
- [ ]
- [ ]
- [ ]
- [ ]
- [ ]
- [ ]
- [ ]
- [ ]

Transactions

Category	Amount
	$
	$
	$
	$
	$

Transactions

Category	Amount
	$
	$
	$
	$
	$

Transactions

Category	Amount
	$
	$
	$
	$
	$

January 8 - 14

8 Sunday	9 Monday	10 Tuesday	11 Wednesday
7am			
8am			
9am			
10am			
11am			
12pm			
1pm			
2pm			
3pm			
4pm			
5pm			
6pm			
7pm			

Transactions

Category	Amount
	$
	$
	$
	$
	$

Transactions

Category	Amount
	$
	$
	$
	$
	$

Transactions

Category	Amount
	$
	$
	$
	$
	$

Transactions

Category	Amount
	$
	$
	$
	$
	$

12 Thursday

13 Friday

14 Saturday

To Do List

Transactions

Category	Amount
	$
	$
	$
	$
	$

Transactions

Category	Amount
	$
	$
	$
	$
	$

Transactions

Category	Amount
	$
	$
	$
	$
	$

January 15 - 21

15 Sunday	16 Monday	17 Tuesday	18 Wednesday
7am			
8am			
9am			
10am			
11am			
12pm			
1pm			
2pm			
3pm			
4pm			
5pm			
6pm			
7pm			

Transactions

Category	Amount
	$
	$
	$
	$
	$

Transactions

Category	Amount
	$
	$
	$
	$
	$

Transactions

Category	Amount
	$
	$
	$
	$
	$

Transactions

Category	Amount
	$
	$
	$
	$
	$

19 Thursday

20 Friday

21 Saturday

To Do List

- [ ]
- [ ]
- [ ]
- [ ]
- [ ]
- [ ]
- [ ]
- [ ]
- [ ]
- [ ]
- [ ]
- [ ]
- [ ]
- [ ]
- [ ]
- [ ]
- [ ]
- [ ]
- [ ]
- [ ]
- [ ]
- [ ]
- [ ]
- [ ]
- [ ]
- [ ]
- [ ]
- [ ]
- [ ]
- [ ]
- [ ]
- [ ]
- [ ]
- [ ]

Transactions

Category	Amount
	$
	$
	$
	$
	$

Transactions

Category	Amount
	$
	$
	$
	$
	$

Transactions

Category	Amount
	$
	$
	$
	$
	$

January 22 - 28

22 Sunday	23 Monday	24 Tuesday	25 Wednesday
7am			
8am			
9am			
10am			
11am			
12pm			
1pm			
2pm			
3pm			
4pm			
5pm			
6pm			
7pm			

Transactions

Category	Amount	Category	Amount	Category	Amount	Category	Amount
	$		$		$		$
	$		$		$		$
	$		$		$		$
	$		$		$		$
	$		$		$		$

26 Thursday

27 Friday

28 Saturday

To Do List

☐
☐
☐
☐
☐
☐
☐
☐
☐
☐
☐
☐
☐
☐
☐
☐
☐
☐
☐
☐
☐
☐
☐
☐
☐
☐
☐
☐
☐
☐
☐
☐
☐
☐

Transactions

Category	Amount
	$
	$
	$
	$
	$

Transactions

Category	Amount
	$
	$
	$
	$
	$

Transactions

Category	Amount
	$
	$
	$
	$
	$

January 29 - 31

29 Sunday	30 Monday	31 Tuesday	1 Wednesday
7am			
8am			
9am			
10am			
11am			
12pm			
1pm			
2pm			
3pm			
4pm			
5pm			
6pm			
7pm			

Transactions

Category	Amount
	$
	$
	$
	$
	$

Transactions

Category	Amount
	$
	$
	$
	$
	$

Transactions

Category	Amount
	$
	$
	$
	$
	$

Transactions

Category	Amount
	$
	$
	$
	$
	$

2 Thursday

3 Friday

4 Saturday

To Do List

- [ ]
- [ ]
- [ ]
- [ ]
- [ ]
- [ ]
- [ ]
- [ ]
- [ ]
- [ ]
- [ ]
- [ ]
- [ ]
- [ ]
- [ ]
- [ ]
- [ ]
- [ ]
- [ ]
- [ ]
- [ ]
- [ ]
- [ ]
- [ ]
- [ ]
- [ ]
- [ ]
- [ ]
- [ ]
- [ ]
- [ ]
- [ ]
- [ ]
- [ ]

Transactions

Category	Amount
	$
	$
	$
	$
	$

Transactions

Category	Amount
	$
	$
	$
	$
	$

Transactions

Category	Amount
	$
	$
	$
	$
	$

FEBRUARY

February's Budget

Income	Projected	Actual
Total Income		

Savings & Investments	Projected	Actual
Total Savings & Investments		

Expenses	Projected	Actual
Total Expenses		

Ending Balance	Projected	Actual
Total Income - Total Savings & Investments - Total Expenses =		

February 1 - 4

29 Sunday

30 Monday

31 Tuesday

1 Wednesday

7am

8am

9am

10am

11am

12pm

1pm

2pm

3pm

4pm

5pm

6pm

7pm

Transactions

Category	Amount
	$
	$
	$
	$
	$

Transactions

Category	Amount
	$
	$
	$
	$
	$

Transactions

Category	Amount
	$
	$
	$
	$
	$

Transactions

Category	Amount
	$
	$
	$
	$
	$

2 Thursday

3 Friday

4 Saturday

To Do List

- [ ]
- [ ]
- [ ]
- [ ]
- [ ]
- [ ]
- [ ]
- [ ]
- [ ]
- [ ]
- [ ]
- [ ]
- [ ]
- [ ]
- [ ]
- [ ]
- [ ]
- [ ]
- [ ]
- [ ]
- [ ]
- [ ]
- [ ]
- [ ]
- [ ]
- [ ]
- [ ]
- [ ]
- [ ]
- [ ]
- [ ]
- [ ]
- [ ]
- [ ]
- [ ]

Transactions

Category	Amount
	$
	$
	$
	$
	$

Transactions

Category	Amount
	$
	$
	$
	$
	$

Transactions

Category	Amount
	$
	$
	$
	$
	$

FEBRUARY 5 - 11

5 SUNDAY	6 MONDAY	7 TUESDAY	8 WEDNESDAY
7am			
8am			
9am			
10am			
11am			
12pm			
1pm			
2pm			
3pm			
4pm			
5pm			
6pm			
7pm			

TRANSACTIONS

Category	Amount
	$
	$
	$
	$
	$

TRANSACTIONS

Category	Amount
	$
	$
	$
	$
	$

TRANSACTIONS

Category	Amount
	$
	$
	$
	$
	$

TRANSACTIONS

Category	Amount
	$
	$
	$
	$
	$

9 Thursday

10 Friday

11 Saturday

To Do List

- [ ]
- [ ]
- [ ]
- [ ]
- [ ]
- [ ]
- [ ]
- [ ]
- [ ]
- [ ]
- [ ]
- [ ]
- [ ]
- [ ]
- [ ]
- [ ]
- [ ]
- [ ]
- [ ]
- [ ]
- [ ]
- [ ]
- [ ]
- [ ]
- [ ]
- [ ]
- [ ]
- [ ]
- [ ]
- [ ]
- [ ]
- [ ]
- [ ]
- [ ]

Transactions

Category	Amount
	$
	$
	$
	$
	$

Transactions

Category	Amount
	$
	$
	$
	$
	$

Transactions

Category	Amount
	$
	$
	$
	$
	$

February 12 - 18

12 Sunday	13 Monday	14 Tuesday	15 Wednesday
7am			
8am			
9am			
10am			
11am			
12pm			
1pm			
2pm			
3pm			
4pm			
5pm			
6pm			
7pm			

Transactions

Category	Amount
	$
	$
	$
	$
	$

Transactions

Category	Amount
	$
	$
	$
	$
	$

Transactions

Category	Amount
	$
	$
	$
	$
	$

Transactions

Category	Amount
	$
	$
	$
	$
	$

16 Thursday

17 Friday

18 Saturday

To Do List

- [ ]
- [ ]
- [ ]

Transactions

Category	Amount
	$
	$
	$
	$
	$

Transactions

Category	Amount
	$
	$
	$
	$
	$

Transactions

Category	Amount
	$
	$
	$
	$
	$

February 19 - 25

19 Sunday	20 Monday	21 Tuesday	22 Wednesday
7am			
8am			
9am			
10am			
11am			
12pm			
1pm			
2pm			
3pm			
4pm			
5pm			
6pm			
7pm			

Transactions

Category	Amount
	$
	$
	$
	$
	$

Transactions

Category	Amount
	$
	$
	$
	$
	$

Transactions

Category	Amount
	$
	$
	$
	$
	$

Transactions

Category	Amount
	$
	$
	$
	$
	$

23 Thursday

24 Friday

25 Saturday

To Do List

- [ ]
- [ ]
- [ ]

Transactions

Category	Amount
	$
	$
	$
	$
	$

Transactions

Category	Amount
	$
	$
	$
	$
	$

Transactions

Category	Amount
	$
	$
	$
	$
	$

FEBRUARY 26 - 28

26 SUNDAY	27 MONDAY	28 TUESDAY	1 WEDNESDAY
7am			
8am			
9am			
10am			
11am			
12pm			
1pm			
2pm			
3pm			
4pm			
5pm			
6pm			
7pm			

TRANSACTIONS

Category	Amount
	$
	$
	$
	$
	$

TRANSACTIONS

Category	Amount
	$
	$
	$
	$
	$

TRANSACTIONS

Category	Amount
	$
	$
	$
	$
	$

TRANSACTIONS

Category	Amount
	$
	$
	$
	$
	$

2 Thursday

3 Friday

4 Saturday

To Do List

- [ ]
- [ ]
- [ ]
- [ ]
- [ ]
- [ ]
- [ ]
- [ ]
- [ ]
- [ ]
- [ ]
- [ ]
- [ ]
- [ ]
- [ ]
- [ ]
- [ ]
- [ ]
- [ ]
- [ ]
- [ ]
- [ ]
- [ ]
- [ ]
- [ ]
- [ ]
- [ ]
- [ ]
- [ ]
- [ ]
- [ ]
- [ ]
- [ ]
- [ ]

Transactions

Category	Amount
	$
	$
	$
	$
	$

Transactions

Category	Amount
	$
	$
	$
	$
	$

Transactions

Category	Amount
	$
	$
	$
	$
	$

MARCH

March's Budget

Income	Projected	Actual
Total Income		

Savings & Investments	Projected	Actual
Total Savings & Investments		

Expenses	Projected	Actual
Total Expenses		

Ending Balance	Projected	Actual
Total Income - Total Savings & Investments - Total Expenses =		

March 1 - 4

26 Sunday

27 Monday

28 Tuesday

1 Wednesday

7am

8am

9am

10am

11am

12pm

1pm

2pm

3pm

4pm

5pm

6pm

7pm

Transactions

Category	Amount
	$
	$
	$
	$
	$

Transactions

Category	Amount
	$
	$
	$
	$
	$

Transactions

Category	Amount
	$
	$
	$
	$
	$

Transactions

Category	Amount
	$
	$
	$
	$
	$

2 Thursday

3 Friday

4 Saturday

To Do List

- ☐
- ☐
- ☐
- ☐
- ☐
- ☐
- ☐
- ☐
- ☐
- ☐
- ☐
- ☐
- ☐
- ☐
- ☐
- ☐
- ☐
- ☐
- ☐
- ☐
- ☐
- ☐
- ☐
- ☐
- ☐
- ☐
- ☐
- ☐
- ☐
- ☐
- ☐
- ☐
- ☐
- ☐

Transactions

Category	Amount
	$
	$
	$
	$
	$

Transactions

Category	Amount
	$
	$
	$
	$
	$

Transactions

Category	Amount
	$
	$
	$
	$
	$

March 5 - 11

5 Sunday

7am

8am

9am

10am

11am

12pm

1pm

2pm

3pm

4pm

5pm

6pm

7pm

6 Monday

7 Tuesday

8 Wednesday

Transactions

Category	Amount
	$
	$
	$
	$
	$

Transactions

Category	Amount
	$
	$
	$
	$
	$

Transactions

Category	Amount
	$
	$
	$
	$
	$

Transactions

Category	Amount
	$
	$
	$
	$
	$

9 Thursday

10 Friday

11 Saturday

To Do List

- ☐
- ☐
- ☐
- ☐
- ☐
- ☐
- ☐
- ☐
- ☐
- ☐
- ☐
- ☐
- ☐
- ☐
- ☐
- ☐
- ☐
- ☐
- ☐
- ☐
- ☐
- ☐
- ☐
- ☐
- ☐
- ☐
- ☐
- ☐
- ☐
- ☐
- ☐
- ☐
- ☐
- ☐

Transactions

Category	Amount
	$
	$
	$
	$
	$

Transactions

Category	Amount
	$
	$
	$
	$
	$

Transactions

Category	Amount
	$
	$
	$
	$
	$

March 12 - 18

12 Sunday	13 Monday	14 Tuesday	15 Wednesday
7am			
8am			
9am			
10am			
11am			
12pm			
1pm			
2pm			
3pm			
4pm			
5pm			
6pm			
7pm			

Transactions

Category	Amount
	$
	$
	$
	$
	$

Transactions

Category	Amount
	$
	$
	$
	$
	$

Transactions

Category	Amount
	$
	$
	$
	$
	$

Transactions

Category	Amount
	$
	$
	$
	$
	$

16 Thursday

17 Friday

18 Saturday

To Do List

- ☐
- ☐
- ☐
- ☐
- ☐
- ☐
- ☐
- ☐
- ☐
- ☐
- ☐
- ☐
- ☐
- ☐
- ☐
- ☐
- ☐
- ☐
- ☐
- ☐
- ☐
- ☐
- ☐
- ☐
- ☐
- ☐
- ☐
- ☐
- ☐
- ☐
- ☐
- ☐
- ☐
- ☐

Transactions

Category	Amount
	$
	$
	$
	$
	$

Transactions

Category	Amount
	$
	$
	$
	$
	$

Transactions

Category	Amount
	$
	$
	$
	$
	$

March 19 - 25

19 Sunday	20 Monday	21 Tuesday	22 Wednesday
7am			
8am			
9am			
10am			
11am			
12pm			
1pm			
2pm			
3pm			
4pm			
5pm			
6pm			
7pm			

Transactions

Category	Amount
	$
	$
	$
	$
	$

Transactions

Category	Amount
	$
	$
	$
	$
	$

Transactions

Category	Amount
	$
	$
	$
	$
	$

Transactions

Category	Amount
	$
	$
	$
	$
	$

23 Thursday

24 Friday

25 Saturday

To Do List

- ☐
- ☐
- ☐
- ☐
- ☐
- ☐
- ☐
- ☐
- ☐
- ☐
- ☐
- ☐
- ☐
- ☐
- ☐
- ☐
- ☐
- ☐
- ☐
- ☐
- ☐
- ☐
- ☐
- ☐
- ☐
- ☐
- ☐
- ☐
- ☐
- ☐
- ☐
- ☐
- ☐
- ☐

Transactions

Category	Amount
	$
	$
	$
	$
	$

Transactions

Category	Amount
	$
	$
	$
	$
	$

Transactions

Category	Amount
	$
	$
	$
	$
	$

March 26 - 31

26 Sunday	27 Monday	28 Tuesday	29 Wednesday
7am			
8am			
9am			
10am			
11am			
12pm			
1pm			
2pm			
3pm			
4pm			
5pm			
6pm			
7pm			

Transactions

Category	Amount
	$
	$
	$
	$
	$

Transactions

Category	Amount
	$
	$
	$
	$
	$

Transactions

Category	Amount
	$
	$
	$
	$
	$

Transactions

Category	Amount
	$
	$
	$
	$
	$

30 Thursday

31 Friday

1 Saturday

To Do List

- [ ]
- [ ]
- [ ]

Transactions

Category	Amount
	$
	$
	$
	$
	$

Transactions

Category	Amount
	$
	$
	$
	$
	$

Transactions

Category	Amount
	$
	$
	$
	$
	$

April

April's Budget

Income	Projected	Actual
Total Income		

Savings & Investments	Projected	Actual
Total Savings & Investments		

Expenses	Projected	Actual
Total Expenses		

Ending Balance	Projected	Actual
Total Income - Total Savings & Investments - Total Expenses =		

April 1

26 Sunday

27 Monday

28 Tuesday

29 Wednesday

Transactions

Category	Amount
	$
	$
	$
	$
	$

Transactions

Category	Amount
	$
	$
	$
	$
	$

Transactions

Category	Amount
	$
	$
	$
	$
	$

Transactions

Category	Amount
	$
	$
	$
	$
	$

30 Thursday

31 Friday

1 Saturday

To Do List

☐
☐
☐
☐
☐
☐
☐
☐
☐
☐
☐
☐
☐
☐
☐
☐
☐
☐
☐
☐
☐
☐
☐
☐
☐
☐
☐
☐
☐
☐
☐
☐
☐
☐

Transactions

Category	Amount
	$
	$
	$
	$
	$

Transactions

Category	Amount
	$
	$
	$
	$
	$

Transactions

Category	Amount
	$
	$
	$
	$
	$

April 2 - 8

2 Sunday	3 Monday	4 Tuesday	5 Wednesday
7am			
8am			
9am			
10am			
11am			
12pm			
1pm			
2pm			
3pm			
4pm			
5pm			
6pm			
7pm			

Transactions		Transactions		Transactions		Transactions	
Category	Amount	Category	Amount	Category	Amount	Category	Amount
	$		$		$		$
	$		$		$		$
	$		$		$		$
	$		$		$		$
	$		$		$		$

6 Thursday

7 Friday

8 Saturday

To Do List

- [ ]
- [ ]
- [ ]
- [ ]
- [ ]
- [ ]
- [ ]
- [ ]
- [ ]
- [ ]
- [ ]
- [ ]
- [ ]
- [ ]
- [ ]
- [ ]
- [ ]
- [ ]
- [ ]
- [ ]
- [ ]
- [ ]
- [ ]
- [ ]
- [ ]
- [ ]
- [ ]
- [ ]
- [ ]
- [ ]
- [ ]
- [ ]
- [ ]
- [ ]
- [ ]

Transactions

Category	Amount
	$
	$
	$
	$
	$

Transactions

Category	Amount
	$
	$
	$
	$
	$

Transactions

Category	Amount
	$
	$
	$
	$
	$

April 9 - 15

9 Sunday	10 Monday	11 Tuesday	12 Wednesday
7am			
8am			
9am			
10am			
11am			
12pm			
1pm			
2pm			
3pm			
4pm			
5pm			
6pm			
7pm			

Transactions

Category	Amount
	$
	$
	$
	$
	$

Transactions

Category	Amount
	$
	$
	$
	$
	$

Transactions

Category	Amount
	$
	$
	$
	$
	$

Transactions

Category	Amount
	$
	$
	$
	$
	$

13 Thursday

14 Friday

15 Saturday

To Do List

- ☐
- ☐
- ☐
- ☐
- ☐
- ☐
- ☐
- ☐
- ☐
- ☐
- ☐
- ☐
- ☐
- ☐
- ☐
- ☐
- ☐
- ☐
- ☐
- ☐
- ☐
- ☐
- ☐
- ☐
- ☐
- ☐
- ☐
- ☐
- ☐
- ☐
- ☐
- ☐
- ☐
- ☐

Transactions

Category	Amount
	$
	$
	$
	$
	$

Transactions

Category	Amount
	$
	$
	$
	$
	$

Transactions

Category	Amount
	$
	$
	$
	$
	$

April 16 - 22

16 Sunday	17 Monday	18 Tuesday	19 Wednesday
7am			
8am			
9am			
10am			
11am			
12pm			
1pm			
2pm			
3pm			
4pm			
5pm			
6pm			
7pm			

Transactions

Category	Amount
	$
	$
	$
	$
	$

Transactions

Category	Amount
	$
	$
	$
	$
	$

Transactions

Category	Amount
	$
	$
	$
	$
	$

Transactions

Category	Amount
	$
	$
	$
	$
	$

20 Thursday

21 Friday

22 Saturday

To Do List

- ☐
- ☐
- ☐
- ☐
- ☐
- ☐
- ☐
- ☐
- ☐
- ☐
- ☐
- ☐
- ☐
- ☐
- ☐
- ☐
- ☐
- ☐
- ☐
- ☐
- ☐
- ☐
- ☐
- ☐
- ☐
- ☐
- ☐
- ☐
- ☐
- ☐
- ☐
- ☐
- ☐
- ☐

Transactions

Category	Amount
	$
	$
	$
	$
	$

Transactions

Category	Amount
	$
	$
	$
	$
	$

Transactions

Category	Amount
	$
	$
	$
	$
	$

April 23 - 29

23 Sunday	24 Monday	25 Tuesday	26 Wednesday
7am			
8am			
9am			
10am			
11am			
12pm			
1pm			
2pm			
3pm			
4pm			
5pm			
6pm			
7pm			

Transactions		Transactions		Transactions		Transactions	
Category	Amount	Category	Amount	Category	Amount	Category	Amount
	$		$		$		$
	$		$		$		$
	$		$		$		$
	$		$		$		$
	$		$		$		$

27 Thursday

28 Friday

29 Saturday

To Do List

- ☐
- ☐
- ☐
- ☐
- ☐
- ☐
- ☐
- ☐
- ☐
- ☐
- ☐
- ☐
- ☐
- ☐
- ☐
- ☐
- ☐
- ☐
- ☐
- ☐
- ☐
- ☐
- ☐
- ☐
- ☐
- ☐
- ☐
- ☐
- ☐
- ☐
- ☐
- ☐
- ☐
- ☐

Transactions

Category	Amount
	$
	$
	$
	$
	$

Transactions

Category	Amount
	$
	$
	$
	$
	$

Transactions

Category	Amount
	$
	$
	$
	$
	$

April 30

30 Sunday	1 Monday	2 Tuesday	3 Wednesday
7am			
8am			
9am			
10am			
11am			
12pm			
1pm			
2pm			
3pm			
4pm			
5pm			
6pm			
7pm			

Transactions

Category	Amount
	$
	$
	$
	$
	$

Transactions

Category	Amount
	$
	$
	$
	$
	$

Transactions

Category	Amount
	$
	$
	$
	$
	$

Transactions

Category	Amount
	$
	$
	$
	$
	$

4 Thursday

5 Friday

6 Saturday

To Do List

- ☐
- ☐
- ☐
- ☐
- ☐
- ☐
- ☐
- ☐
- ☐
- ☐
- ☐
- ☐
- ☐
- ☐
- ☐
- ☐
- ☐
- ☐
- ☐
- ☐
- ☐
- ☐
- ☐
- ☐
- ☐
- ☐
- ☐
- ☐
- ☐
- ☐
- ☐
- ☐
- ☐
- ☐

Transactions

Category	Amount
	$
	$
	$
	$
	$

Transactions

Category	Amount
	$
	$
	$
	$
	$

Transactions

Category	Amount
	$
	$
	$
	$
	$

May

May's Budget

Income	Projected	Actual
Total Income		

Savings & Investments	Projected	Actual
Total Savings & Investments		

Expenses	Projected	Actual
Total Expenses		

Ending Balance	Projected	Actual
Total Income - Total Savings & Investments - Total Expenses =		

May 1 - 6

30 Sunday	1 Monday	2 Tuesday	3 Wednesday
	7am		
	8am		
	9am		
	10am		
	11am		
	12pm		
	1pm		
	2pm		
	3pm		
	4pm		
	5pm		
	6pm		
	7pm		

Transactions

Category	Amount
	$
	$
	$
	$
	$

Transactions

Category	Amount
	$
	$
	$
	$
	$

Transactions

Category	Amount
	$
	$
	$
	$
	$

Transactions

Category	Amount
	$
	$
	$
	$
	$

4 Thursday

5 Friday

6 Saturday

To Do List

- [ ]
- [ ]
- [ ]
- [ ]
- [ ]
- [ ]
- [ ]
- [ ]
- [ ]
- [ ]
- [ ]
- [ ]
- [ ]
- [ ]
- [ ]
- [ ]
- [ ]
- [ ]
- [ ]
- [ ]
- [ ]
- [ ]
- [ ]
- [ ]
- [ ]
- [ ]
- [ ]
- [ ]
- [ ]
- [ ]
- [ ]
- [ ]
- [ ]
- [ ]
- [ ]

Transactions

Category	Amount
	$
	$
	$
	$
	$

Transactions

Category	Amount
	$
	$
	$
	$
	$

Transactions

Category	Amount
	$
	$
	$
	$
	$

May 7 - 13

7 Sunday	8 Monday	9 Tuesday	10 Wednesday
7am			
8am			
9am			
10am			
11am			
12pm			
1pm			
2pm			
3pm			
4pm			
5pm			
6pm			
7pm			

Transactions

Category	Amount
	$
	$
	$
	$
	$

Transactions

Category	Amount
	$
	$
	$
	$
	$

Transactions

Category	Amount
	$
	$
	$
	$
	$

Transactions

Category	Amount
	$
	$
	$
	$
	$

11 Thursday

12 Friday

13 Saturday

To Do List

☐
☐
☐
☐
☐
☐
☐
☐
☐
☐
☐
☐
☐
☐
☐
☐
☐
☐
☐
☐
☐
☐
☐
☐
☐
☐
☐
☐
☐
☐
☐
☐
☐
☐

Transactions

Category	Amount
	$
	$
	$
	$
	$

Transactions

Category	Amount
	$
	$
	$
	$
	$

Transactions

Category	Amount
	$
	$
	$
	$
	$

May 14 - 20

14 Sunday	15 Monday	16 Tuesday	17 Wednesday
7am			
8am			
9am			
10am			
11am			
12pm			
1pm			
2pm			
3pm			
4pm			
5pm			
6pm			
7pm			

Transactions

Category	Amount
	$
	$
	$
	$
	$

Transactions

Category	Amount
	$
	$
	$
	$
	$

Transactions

Category	Amount
	$
	$
	$
	$
	$

Transactions

Category	Amount
	$
	$
	$
	$
	$

18 Thursday

19 Friday

20 Saturday

To Do List

- [ ]
- [ ]
- [ ]
- [ ]
- [ ]
- [ ]
- [ ]
- [ ]
- [ ]
- [ ]
- [ ]
- [ ]
- [ ]
- [ ]
- [ ]
- [ ]
- [ ]
- [ ]
- [ ]
- [ ]
- [ ]
- [ ]
- [ ]
- [ ]
- [ ]
- [ ]
- [ ]
- [ ]
- [ ]
- [ ]
- [ ]
- [ ]
- [ ]
- [ ]
- [ ]
- [ ]
- [ ]

Transactions

Category	Amount
	$
	$
	$
	$
	$

Transactions

Category	Amount
	$
	$
	$
	$
	$

Transactions

Category	Amount
	$
	$
	$
	$
	$

May 21 - 27

21 Sunday	22 Monday	23 Tuesday	24 Wednesday
7am			
8am			
9am			
10am			
11am			
12pm			
1pm			
2pm			
3pm			
4pm			
5pm			
6pm			
7pm			

Transactions

Category	Amount
	$
	$
	$
	$
	$

Transactions

Category	Amount
	$
	$
	$
	$
	$

Transactions

Category	Amount
	$
	$
	$
	$
	$

Transactions

Category	Amount
	$
	$
	$
	$
	$

25 Thursday

26 Friday

27 Saturday

To Do List

- ☐
- ☐
- ☐
- ☐
- ☐
- ☐
- ☐
- ☐
- ☐
- ☐
- ☐
- ☐
- ☐
- ☐
- ☐
- ☐
- ☐
- ☐
- ☐
- ☐
- ☐
- ☐
- ☐
- ☐
- ☐
- ☐
- ☐
- ☐
- ☐
- ☐
- ☐
- ☐
- ☐
- ☐
- ☐

Transactions

Category	Amount
	$
	$
	$
	$
	$

Transactions

Category	Amount
	$
	$
	$
	$
	$

Transactions

Category	Amount
	$
	$
	$
	$
	$

May 28 - 31

28 Sunday	29 Monday	30 Tuesday	31 Wednesday
7am			
8am			
9am			
10am			
11am			
12pm			
1pm			
2pm			
3pm			
4pm			
5pm			
6pm			
7pm			

Transactions

Category	Amount
	$
	$
	$
	$
	$

Transactions

Category	Amount
	$
	$
	$
	$
	$

Transactions

Category	Amount
	$
	$
	$
	$
	$

Transactions

Category	Amount
	$
	$
	$
	$
	$

1 Thursday

2 Friday

3 Saturday

To Do List

- ☐
- ☐
- ☐
- ☐
- ☐
- ☐
- ☐
- ☐
- ☐
- ☐
- ☐
- ☐
- ☐
- ☐
- ☐
- ☐
- ☐
- ☐
- ☐
- ☐
- ☐
- ☐
- ☐
- ☐
- ☐
- ☐
- ☐
- ☐
- ☐
- ☐
- ☐
- ☐
- ☐
- ☐

Transactions

Category	Amount
	$
	$
	$
	$
	$

Transactions

Category	Amount
	$
	$
	$
	$
	$

Transactions

Category	Amount
	$
	$
	$
	$
	$

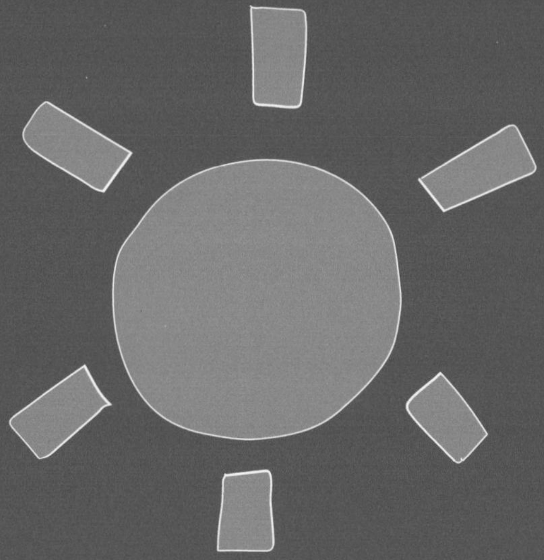

JUNE

June's Budget

Income	Projected	Actual
Total Income		

Savings & Investments	Projected	Actual
Total Savings & Investments		

Expenses	Projected	Actual
Total Expenses		

Ending Balance	Projected	Actual
Total Income - Total Savings & Investments - Total Expenses =		

JUNE 1 - 3

28 SUNDAY

29 MONDAY

30 TUESDAY

31 WEDNESDAY

TRANSACTIONS

Category	Amount
	$
	$
	$
	$
	$

TRANSACTIONS

Category	Amount
	$
	$
	$
	$
	$

TRANSACTIONS

Category	Amount
	$
	$
	$
	$
	$

TRANSACTIONS

Category	Amount
	$
	$
	$
	$
	$

1 Thursday

2 Friday

3 Saturday

To Do List

Transactions

Category	Amount
	$
	$
	$
	$
	$

Transactions

Category	Amount
	$
	$
	$
	$
	$

Transactions

Category	Amount
	$
	$
	$
	$
	$

JUNE 4 - 10

4 SUNDAY	5 MONDAY	6 TUESDAY	7 WEDNESDAY
7am			
8am			
9am			
10am			
11am			
12pm			
1pm			
2pm			
3pm			
4pm			
5pm			
6pm			
7pm			

TRANSACTIONS

Category	Amount
	$
	$
	$
	$
	$

TRANSACTIONS

Category	Amount
	$
	$
	$
	$
	$

TRANSACTIONS

Category	Amount
	$
	$
	$
	$
	$

TRANSACTIONS

Category	Amount
	$
	$
	$
	$
	$

8 Thursday

9 Friday

10 Saturday

To Do List

- ☐
- ☐
- ☐
- ☐
- ☐
- ☐
- ☐
- ☐
- ☐
- ☐
- ☐
- ☐
- ☐
- ☐
- ☐
- ☐
- ☐
- ☐
- ☐
- ☐
- ☐
- ☐
- ☐
- ☐
- ☐
- ☐
- ☐
- ☐
- ☐
- ☐
- ☐
- ☐
- ☐
- ☐

Transactions

Category	Amount
	$
	$
	$
	$
	$

Transactions

Category	Amount
	$
	$
	$
	$
	$

Transactions

Category	Amount
	$
	$
	$
	$
	$

June 11 - 17

11 Sunday	12 Monday	13 Tuesday	14 Wednesday
7am			
8am			
9am			
10am			
11am			
12pm			
1pm			
2pm			
3pm			
4pm			
5pm			
6pm			
7pm			

Transactions

Category	Amount
	$
	$
	$
	$
	$

Transactions

Category	Amount
	$
	$
	$
	$
	$

Transactions

Category	Amount
	$
	$
	$
	$
	$

Transactions

Category	Amount
	$
	$
	$
	$
	$

15 Thursday

16 Friday

17 Saturday

To Do List

- ☐
- ☐
- ☐
- ☐
- ☐
- ☐
- ☐
- ☐
- ☐
- ☐
- ☐
- ☐
- ☐
- ☐
- ☐
- ☐
- ☐
- ☐
- ☐
- ☐
- ☐
- ☐
- ☐
- ☐
- ☐
- ☐
- ☐
- ☐
- ☐
- ☐
- ☐
- ☐
- ☐
- ☐
- ☐

Transactions

Category	Amount
	$
	$
	$
	$
	$

Transactions

Category	Amount
	$
	$
	$
	$
	$

Transactions

Category	Amount
	$
	$
	$
	$
	$

June 18 - 24

18 Sunday	19 Monday	20 Tuesday	21 Wednesday
7am			
8am			
9am			
10am			
11am			
12pm			
1pm			
2pm			
3pm			
4pm			
5pm			
6pm			
7pm			

Transactions

Category	Amount
	$
	$
	$
	$
	$

Transactions

Category	Amount
	$
	$
	$
	$
	$

Transactions

Category	Amount
	$
	$
	$
	$
	$

Transactions

Category	Amount
	$
	$
	$
	$
	$

22 Thursday

23 Friday

24 Saturday

To Do List

- [ ]
- [ ]
- [ ]
- [ ]
- [ ]
- [ ]
- [ ]
- [ ]
- [ ]
- [ ]
- [ ]
- [ ]
- [ ]
- [ ]
- [ ]
- [ ]
- [ ]
- [ ]
- [ ]
- [ ]
- [ ]
- [ ]
- [ ]
- [ ]
- [ ]
- [ ]
- [ ]
- [ ]
- [ ]
- [ ]
- [ ]
- [ ]
- [ ]
- [ ]
- [ ]
- [ ]

Transactions

Category	Amount
	$
	$
	$
	$
	$

Transactions

Category	Amount
	$
	$
	$
	$
	$

Transactions

Category	Amount
	$
	$
	$
	$
	$

☼ June 25 - 30

25 Sunday	26 Monday	27 Tuesday	28 Wednesday
7am			
8am			
9am			
10am			
11am			
12pm			
1pm			
2pm			
3pm			
4pm			
5pm			
6pm			
7pm			

Transactions

Category	Amount
	$
	$
	$
	$
	$

Transactions

Category	Amount
	$
	$
	$
	$
	$

Transactions

Category	Amount
	$
	$
	$
	$
	$

Transactions

Category	Amount
	$
	$
	$
	$
	$

29 Thursday

30 Friday

1 Saturday

To Do List

- [ ]
- [ ]
- [ ]
- [ ]
- [ ]
- [ ]
- [ ]
- [ ]
- [ ]
- [ ]
- [ ]
- [ ]
- [ ]
- [ ]
- [ ]
- [ ]
- [ ]
- [ ]
- [ ]
- [ ]
- [ ]
- [ ]
- [ ]
- [ ]
- [ ]
- [ ]
- [ ]
- [ ]
- [ ]
- [ ]
- [ ]
- [ ]
- [ ]
- [ ]
- [ ]
- [ ]

Transactions

Category	Amount
	$
	$
	$
	$
	$

Transactions

Category	Amount
	$
	$
	$
	$
	$

Transactions

Category	Amount
	$
	$
	$
	$
	$

July

July's Budget

Income	Projected	Actual
Total Income		

Savings & Investments	Projected	Actual
Total Savings & Investments		

Expenses	Projected	Actual
Total Expenses		

Ending Balance	Projected	Actual
Total Income - Total Savings & Investments - Total Expenses =		

July 1

25 Sunday

26 Monday

27 Tuesday

28 Wednesday

Transactions

Category	Amount
	$
	$
	$
	$
	$

Transactions

Category	Amount
	$
	$
	$
	$
	$

Transactions

Category	Amount
	$
	$
	$
	$
	$

Transactions

Category	Amount
	$
	$
	$
	$
	$

29 Thursday

30 Friday

1 Saturday

To Do List

- ☐
- ☐
- ☐
- ☐
- ☐
- ☐
- ☐
- ☐
- ☐
- ☐
- ☐
- ☐
- ☐
- ☐
- ☐
- ☐
- ☐
- ☐
- ☐
- ☐
- ☐
- ☐
- ☐
- ☐
- ☐
- ☐
- ☐
- ☐
- ☐
- ☐
- ☐
- ☐
- ☐
- ☐

Transactions

Category	Amount
	$
	$
	$
	$
	$

Transactions

Category	Amount
	$
	$
	$
	$
	$

Transactions

Category	Amount
	$
	$
	$
	$
	$

JULY 2 - 8

2 SUNDAY	3 MONDAY	4 TUESDAY	5 WEDNESDAY
7am			
8am			
9am			
10am			
11am			
12pm			
1pm			
2pm			
3pm			
4pm			
5pm			
6pm			
7pm			

TRANSACTIONS		TRANSACTIONS		TRANSACTIONS		TRANSACTIONS	
Category	Amount	Category	Amount	Category	Amount	Category	Amount
	$		$		$		$
	$		$		$		$
	$		$		$		$
	$		$		$		$
	$		$		$		$

6 Thursday

7 Friday

8 Saturday

To Do List

☐
☐
☐
☐
☐
☐
☐
☐
☐
☐
☐
☐
☐
☐
☐
☐
☐
☐
☐
☐
☐
☐
☐
☐
☐
☐
☐
☐
☐
☐
☐
☐
☐
☐
☐
☐
☐

Transactions

Category	Amount
	$
	$
	$
	$
	$

Transactions

Category	Amount
	$
	$
	$
	$
	$

Transactions

Category	Amount
	$
	$
	$
	$
	$

July 9 - 15

9 Sunday	10 Monday	11 Tuesday	12 Wednesday
7am			
8am			
9am			
10am			
11am			
12pm			
1pm			
2pm			
3pm			
4pm			
5pm			
6pm			
7pm			

Transactions		Transactions		Transactions		Transactions	
Category	Amount	Category	Amount	Category	Amount	Category	Amount
	$		$		$		$
	$		$		$		$
	$		$		$		$
	$		$		$		$
	$		$		$		$

13 Thursday

14 Friday

15 Saturday

To Do List

Transactions

Category	Amount
	$
	$
	$
	$
	$

Transactions

Category	Amount
	$
	$
	$
	$
	$

Transactions

Category	Amount
	$
	$
	$
	$
	$

July 16 - 22

16 Sunday

7am	
8am	
9am	
10am	
11am	
12pm	
1pm	
2pm	
3pm	
4pm	
5pm	
6pm	
7pm	

17 Monday

18 Tuesday

19 Wednesday

Transactions

Category	Amount
	$
	$
	$
	$
	$

Transactions

Category	Amount
	$
	$
	$
	$
	$

Transactions

Category	Amount
	$
	$
	$
	$
	$

Transactions

Category	Amount
	$
	$
	$
	$
	$

20 Thursday

21 Friday

22 Saturday

To Do List

☐
☐
☐
☐
☐
☐
☐
☐
☐
☐
☐
☐
☐
☐
☐
☐
☐
☐
☐
☐
☐
☐
☐
☐
☐
☐
☐
☐
☐
☐
☐
☐
☐
☐

Transactions

Category	Amount
	$
	$
	$
	$
	$

Transactions

Category	Amount
	$
	$
	$
	$
	$

Transactions

Category	Amount
	$
	$
	$
	$
	$

JULY 23 - 29

23 SUNDAY	24 MONDAY	25 TUESDAY	26 WEDNESDAY
7am			
8am			
9am			
10am			
11am			
12pm			
1pm			
2pm			
3pm			
4pm			
5pm			
6pm			
7pm			

TRANSACTIONS

Category	Amount
	$
	$
	$
	$
	$

TRANSACTIONS

Category	Amount
	$
	$
	$
	$
	$

TRANSACTIONS

Category	Amount
	$
	$
	$
	$
	$

TRANSACTIONS

Category	Amount
	$
	$
	$
	$
	$

27 Thursday

28 Friday

29 Saturday

To Do List

- ☐
- ☐
- ☐
- ☐
- ☐
- ☐
- ☐
- ☐
- ☐
- ☐
- ☐
- ☐
- ☐
- ☐
- ☐
- ☐
- ☐
- ☐
- ☐
- ☐
- ☐
- ☐
- ☐
- ☐
- ☐
- ☐
- ☐
- ☐
- ☐
- ☐
- ☐
- ☐
- ☐
- ☐

Transactions

Category	Amount
	$
	$
	$
	$
	$

Transactions

Category	Amount
	$
	$
	$
	$
	$

Transactions

Category	Amount
	$
	$
	$
	$
	$

JULY 30 - 31

30 SUNDAY	31 MONDAY	1 TUESDAY	2 WEDNESDAY
7am			
8am			
9am			
10am			
11am			
12pm			
1pm			
2pm			
3pm			
4pm			
5pm			
6pm			
7pm			

TRANSACTIONS		TRANSACTIONS		TRANSACTIONS		TRANSACTIONS	
Category	Amount	Category	Amount	Category	Amount	Category	Amount
	$		$		$		$
	$		$		$		$
	$		$		$		$
	$		$		$		$
	$		$		$		$

3 Thursday

Transactions

Category	Amount
	$
	$
	$
	$
	$

4 Friday

Transactions

Category	Amount
	$
	$
	$
	$
	$

5 Saturday

Transactions

Category	Amount
	$
	$
	$
	$
	$

To Do List

- ☐
- ☐
- ☐
- ☐
- ☐
- ☐
- ☐
- ☐
- ☐
- ☐
- ☐
- ☐
- ☐
- ☐
- ☐
- ☐
- ☐
- ☐
- ☐
- ☐
- ☐
- ☐
- ☐
- ☐
- ☐
- ☐
- ☐
- ☐
- ☐
- ☐
- ☐
- ☐
- ☐
- ☐

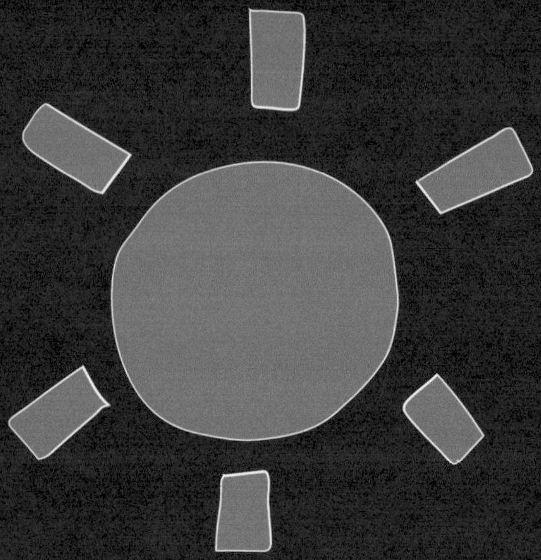

AUGUST

August's Budget

Income	Projected	Actual
Total Income		

Savings & Investments	Projected	Actual
Total Savings & Investments		

Expenses	Projected	Actual
Total Expenses		

Ending Balance	Projected	Actual
Total Income - Total Savings & Investments - Total Expenses =		

AUGUST 1 - 5

30 SUNDAY

31 MONDAY

1 TUESDAY

7am

8am

9am

10am

11am

12pm

1pm

2pm

3pm

4pm

5pm

6pm

7pm

2 WEDNESDAY

TRANSACTIONS

Category	Amount
	$
	$
	$
	$
	$

TRANSACTIONS

Category	Amount
	$
	$
	$
	$
	$

TRANSACTIONS

Category	Amount
	$
	$
	$
	$
	$

TRANSACTIONS

Category	Amount
	$
	$
	$
	$
	$

3 Thursday

4 Friday

5 Saturday

To Do List

- ☐
- ☐
- ☐
- ☐
- ☐
- ☐
- ☐
- ☐
- ☐
- ☐
- ☐
- ☐
- ☐
- ☐
- ☐
- ☐
- ☐
- ☐
- ☐
- ☐
- ☐
- ☐
- ☐
- ☐
- ☐
- ☐
- ☐
- ☐
- ☐
- ☐
- ☐
- ☐
- ☐
- ☐
- ☐

Transactions

Category	Amount
	$
	$
	$
	$
	$

Transactions

Category	Amount
	$
	$
	$
	$
	$

Transactions

Category	Amount
	$
	$
	$
	$
	$

August 6 - 12

6 Sunday	7 Monday	8 Tuesday	9 Wednesday
7am			
8am			
9am			
10am			
11am			
12pm			
1pm			
2pm			
3pm			
4pm			
5pm			
6pm			
7pm			

Transactions

Category	Amount
	$
	$
	$
	$
	$

Transactions

Category	Amount
	$
	$
	$
	$
	$

Transactions

Category	Amount
	$
	$
	$
	$
	$

Transactions

Category	Amount
	$
	$
	$
	$
	$

10 Thursday

11 Friday

12 Saturday

To Do List

- [ ]
- [ ]
- [ ]

Transactions

Category	Amount
	$
	$
	$
	$
	$

Transactions

Category	Amount
	$
	$
	$
	$
	$

Transactions

Category	Amount
	$
	$
	$
	$
	$

AUGUST 13 - 19

13 SUNDAY	14 MONDAY	15 TUESDAY	16 WEDNESDAY
7am			
8am			
9am			
10am			
11am			
12pm			
1pm			
2pm			
3pm			
4pm			
5pm			
6pm			
7pm			

TRANSACTIONS

Category	Amount
	$
	$
	$
	$
	$

TRANSACTIONS

Category	Amount
	$
	$
	$
	$
	$

TRANSACTIONS

Category	Amount
	$
	$
	$
	$
	$

TRANSACTIONS

Category	Amount
	$
	$
	$
	$
	$

17 Thursday

18 Friday

19 Saturday

To Do List

- ☐
- ☐
- ☐
- ☐
- ☐
- ☐
- ☐
- ☐
- ☐
- ☐
- ☐
- ☐
- ☐
- ☐
- ☐
- ☐
- ☐
- ☐
- ☐
- ☐
- ☐
- ☐
- ☐
- ☐
- ☐
- ☐
- ☐
- ☐
- ☐
- ☐
- ☐
- ☐
- ☐
- ☐

Transactions

Category	Amount
	$
	$
	$
	$
	$

Transactions

Category	Amount
	$
	$
	$
	$
	$

Transactions

Category	Amount
	$
	$
	$
	$
	$

August 20 - 26

20 Sunday	21 Monday	22 Tuesday	23 Wednesday
7am			
8am			
9am			
10am			
11am			
12pm			
1pm			
2pm			
3pm			
4pm			
5pm			
6pm			
7pm			

Transactions

Category	Amount
	$
	$
	$
	$
	$

Transactions

Category	Amount
	$
	$
	$
	$
	$

Transactions

Category	Amount
	$
	$
	$
	$
	$

Transactions

Category	Amount
	$
	$
	$
	$
	$

24 Thursday

25 Friday

26 Saturday

To Do List

- ☐
- ☐
- ☐
- ☐
- ☐
- ☐
- ☐
- ☐
- ☐
- ☐
- ☐
- ☐
- ☐
- ☐
- ☐
- ☐
- ☐
- ☐
- ☐
- ☐
- ☐
- ☐
- ☐
- ☐
- ☐
- ☐
- ☐
- ☐
- ☐
- ☐
- ☐
- ☐
- ☐
- ☐
- ☐

Transactions

Category	Amount
	$
	$
	$
	$
	$

Transactions

Category	Amount
	$
	$
	$
	$
	$

Transactions

Category	Amount
	$
	$
	$
	$
	$

August 27 - 31

27 Sunday

Time	
7am	
8am	
9am	
10am	
11am	
12pm	
1pm	
2pm	
3pm	
4pm	
5pm	
6pm	
7pm	

28 Monday

29 Tuesday

30 Wednesday

Transactions

Category	Amount
	$
	$
	$
	$
	$

Transactions

Category	Amount
	$
	$
	$
	$
	$

Transactions

Category	Amount
	$
	$
	$
	$
	$

Transactions

Category	Amount
	$
	$
	$
	$
	$

31 Thursday

1 Friday

2 Saturday

To Do List

☐
☐
☐
☐
☐
☐
☐
☐
☐
☐
☐
☐
☐
☐
☐
☐
☐
☐
☐
☐
☐
☐
☐
☐
☐
☐
☐
☐
☐
☐
☐
☐
☐
☐

Transactions

Category	Amount
	$
	$
	$
	$
	$

Transactions

Category	Amount
	$
	$
	$
	$
	$

Transactions

Category	Amount
	$
	$
	$
	$
	$

SEPTEMBER

September's Budget

Income	Projected	Actual
Total Income		

Savings & Investments	Projected	Actual
Total Savings & Investments		

Expenses	Projected	Actual
Total Expenses		

Ending Balance	Projected	Actual
Total Income - Total Savings & Investments - Total Expenses =		

SEPTEMBER 1 - 2

27 SUNDAY

28 MONDAY

29 TUESDAY

30 WEDNESDAY

TRANSACTIONS

Category	Amount
	$
	$
	$
	$
	$

TRANSACTIONS

Category	Amount
	$
	$
	$
	$
	$

TRANSACTIONS

Category	Amount
	$
	$
	$
	$
	$

TRANSACTIONS

Category	Amount
	$
	$
	$
	$
	$

31 Thursday

1 Friday

2 Saturday

To Do List

- [ ]
- [ ]
- [ ]
- [ ]
- [ ]
- [ ]
- [ ]
- [ ]
- [ ]
- [ ]
- [ ]
- [ ]
- [ ]
- [ ]
- [ ]
- [ ]
- [ ]
- [ ]
- [ ]
- [ ]
- [ ]
- [ ]
- [ ]
- [ ]
- [ ]
- [ ]
- [ ]
- [ ]
- [ ]
- [ ]
- [ ]
- [ ]
- [ ]
- [ ]

Transactions

Category	Amount
	$
	$
	$
	$
	$

Transactions

Category	Amount
	$
	$
	$
	$
	$

Transactions

Category	Amount
	$
	$
	$
	$
	$

September 3 - 9

3 Sunday	4 Monday	5 Tuesday	6 Wednesday
7am			
8am			
9am			
10am			
11am			
12pm			
1pm			
2pm			
3pm			
4pm			
5pm			
6pm			
7pm			

Transactions

Category	Amount
	$
	$
	$
	$
	$

Transactions

Category	Amount
	$
	$
	$
	$
	$

Transactions

Category	Amount
	$
	$
	$
	$
	$

Transactions

Category	Amount
	$
	$
	$
	$
	$

7 Thursday

8 Friday

9 Saturday

To Do List

Transactions

Category	Amount
	$
	$
	$
	$
	$

Transactions

Category	Amount
	$
	$
	$
	$
	$

Transactions

Category	Amount
	$
	$
	$
	$
	$

SEPTEMBER 10 - 16

10 SUNDAY	11 MONDAY	12 TUESDAY	13 WEDNESDAY
7am			
8am			
9am			
10am			
11am			
12pm			
1pm			
2pm			
3pm			
4pm			
5pm			
6pm			
7pm			

TRANSACTIONS	
Category	Amount
	$
	$
	$
	$
	$

TRANSACTIONS	
Category	Amount
	$
	$
	$
	$
	$

TRANSACTIONS	
Category	Amount
	$
	$
	$
	$
	$

TRANSACTIONS	
Category	Amount
	$
	$
	$
	$
	$

14 Thursday

15 Friday

16 Saturday

To Do List

☐
☐
☐
☐
☐
☐
☐
☐
☐
☐
☐
☐
☐
☐
☐
☐
☐
☐
☐
☐
☐
☐
☐
☐
☐
☐
☐
☐
☐
☐
☐
☐
☐
☐

Transactions

Category	Amount
	$
	$
	$
	$
	$

Transactions

Category	Amount
	$
	$
	$
	$
	$

Transactions

Category	Amount
	$
	$
	$
	$
	$

September 17 - 23

17 Sunday	18 Monday	19 Tuesday	20 Wednesday
7am			
8am			
9am			
10am			
11am			
12pm			
1pm			
2pm			
3pm			
4pm			
5pm			
6pm			
7pm			

Transactions

Category	Amount
	$
	$
	$
	$
	$

Transactions

Category	Amount
	$
	$
	$
	$
	$

Transactions

Category	Amount
	$
	$
	$
	$
	$

Transactions

Category	Amount
	$
	$
	$
	$
	$

21 Thursday

22 Friday

23 Saturday

To Do List

- [ ]
- [ ]
- [ ]
- [ ]
- [ ]
- [ ]
- [ ]
- [ ]
- [ ]
- [ ]
- [ ]
- [ ]
- [ ]
- [ ]
- [ ]
- [ ]
- [ ]
- [ ]
- [ ]
- [ ]
- [ ]
- [ ]
- [ ]
- [ ]
- [ ]
- [ ]
- [ ]
- [ ]
- [ ]
- [ ]
- [ ]
- [ ]
- [ ]
- [ ]

Transactions

Category	Amount
	$
	$
	$
	$
	$

Transactions

Category	Amount
	$
	$
	$
	$
	$

Transactions

Category	Amount
	$
	$
	$
	$
	$

September 24 - 30

24 Sunday	25 Monday	26 Tuesday	27 Wednesday
7am			
8am			
9am			
10am			
11am			
12pm			
1pm			
2pm			
3pm			
4pm			
5pm			
6pm			
7pm			

Transactions

Category	Amount
	$
	$
	$
	$
	$

Transactions

Category	Amount
	$
	$
	$
	$
	$

Transactions

Category	Amount
	$
	$
	$
	$
	$

Transactions

Category	Amount
	$
	$
	$
	$
	$

28 Thursday

29 Friday

30 Saturday

To Do List

- [ ]
- [ ]
- [ ]
- [ ]
- [ ]
- [ ]
- [ ]
- [ ]
- [ ]
- [ ]
- [ ]
- [ ]
- [ ]
- [ ]
- [ ]
- [ ]
- [ ]
- [ ]
- [ ]
- [ ]
- [ ]
- [ ]
- [ ]
- [ ]
- [ ]
- [ ]
- [ ]
- [ ]
- [ ]
- [ ]
- [ ]
- [ ]
- [ ]
- [ ]

Transactions

Category	Amount
	$
	$
	$
	$
	$

Transactions

Category	Amount
	$
	$
	$
	$
	$

Transactions

Category	Amount
	$
	$
	$
	$
	$

OCTOBER

October's Budget

Income	Projected	Actual
Total Income		

Savings & Investments	Projected	Actual
Total Savings & Investments		

Expenses	Projected	Actual
Total Expenses		

Ending Balance	Projected	Actual
Total Income - Total Savings & Investments - Total Expenses =		

October 1 - 7

1 Sunday	2 Monday	3 Tuesday	4 Wednesday
7am			
8am			
9am			
10am			
11am			
12pm			
1pm			
2pm			
3pm			
4pm			
5pm			
6pm			
7pm			

Transactions		Transactions		Transactions		Transactions	
Category	Amount	Category	Amount	Category	Amount	Category	Amount
	$		$		$		$
	$		$		$		$
	$		$		$		$
	$		$		$		$
	$		$		$		$

5 Thursday

6 Friday

7 Saturday

To Do List

- [ ]
- [ ]
- [ ]
- [ ]
- [ ]
- [ ]
- [ ]
- [ ]
- [ ]
- [ ]
- [ ]
- [ ]
- [ ]
- [ ]
- [ ]
- [ ]
- [ ]
- [ ]
- [ ]
- [ ]
- [ ]
- [ ]
- [ ]
- [ ]
- [ ]
- [ ]
- [ ]
- [ ]
- [ ]
- [ ]
- [ ]
- [ ]
- [ ]
- [ ]
- [ ]

Transactions

Category	Amount
	$
	$
	$
	$
	$

Transactions

Category	Amount
	$
	$
	$
	$
	$

Transactions

Category	Amount
	$
	$
	$
	$
	$

October 8 - 14

8 Sunday	9 Monday	10 Tuesday	11 Wednesday
7am			
8am			
9am			
10am			
11am			
12pm			
1pm			
2pm			
3pm			
4pm			
5pm			
6pm			
7pm			

Transactions

Category	Amount
	$
	$
	$
	$
	$

Transactions

Category	Amount
	$
	$
	$
	$
	$

Transactions

Category	Amount
	$
	$
	$
	$
	$

Transactions

Category	Amount
	$
	$
	$
	$
	$

12 Thursday

13 Friday

14 Saturday

To Do List

- ☐
- ☐
- ☐
- ☐
- ☐
- ☐
- ☐
- ☐
- ☐
- ☐
- ☐
- ☐
- ☐
- ☐
- ☐
- ☐
- ☐
- ☐
- ☐
- ☐
- ☐
- ☐
- ☐
- ☐
- ☐
- ☐
- ☐
- ☐
- ☐
- ☐
- ☐
- ☐
- ☐
- ☐
- ☐

Transactions

Category	Amount
	$
	$
	$
	$
	$

Transactions

Category	Amount
	$
	$
	$
	$
	$

Transactions

Category	Amount
	$
	$
	$
	$
	$

October 15 - 21

15 Sunday	16 Monday	17 Tuesday	18 Wednesday
7am			
8am			
9am			
10am			
11am			
12pm			
1pm			
2pm			
3pm			
4pm			
5pm			
6pm			
7pm			

Transactions

Category	Amount
	$
	$
	$
	$
	$

Transactions

Category	Amount
	$
	$
	$
	$
	$

Transactions

Category	Amount
	$
	$
	$
	$
	$

Transactions

Category	Amount
	$
	$
	$
	$
	$

19 Thursday

20 Friday

21 Saturday

To Do List

☐
☐
☐
☐
☐
☐
☐
☐
☐
☐
☐
☐
☐
☐
☐
☐
☐
☐
☐
☐
☐
☐
☐
☐
☐
☐
☐
☐
☐
☐
☐
☐
☐
☐

Transactions

Category	Amount
	$
	$
	$
	$
	$

Transactions

Category	Amount
	$
	$
	$
	$
	$

Transactions

Category	Amount
	$
	$
	$
	$
	$

October 22 - 28

22 Sunday	23 Monday	24 Tuesday	25 Wednesday
7am			
8am			
9am			
10am			
11am			
12pm			
1pm			
2pm			
3pm			
4pm			
5pm			
6pm			
7pm			

Transactions

Category	Amount
	$
	$
	$
	$
	$

Transactions

Category	Amount
	$
	$
	$
	$
	$

Transactions

Category	Amount
	$
	$
	$
	$
	$

Transactions

Category	Amount
	$
	$
	$
	$
	$

26 Thursday

27 Friday

28 Saturday

To Do List

- [ ]
- [ ]
- [ ]
- [ ]
- [ ]
- [ ]
- [ ]
- [ ]
- [ ]
- [ ]
- [ ]
- [ ]
- [ ]
- [ ]
- [ ]
- [ ]
- [ ]
- [ ]
- [ ]
- [ ]
- [ ]
- [ ]
- [ ]
- [ ]
- [ ]
- [ ]
- [ ]
- [ ]
- [ ]
- [ ]
- [ ]
- [ ]
- [ ]
- [ ]

Transactions

Category	Amount
	$
	$
	$
	$
	$

Transactions

Category	Amount
	$
	$
	$
	$
	$

Transactions

Category	Amount
	$
	$
	$
	$
	$

October 29 - 31

29 Sunday	30 Monday	31 Tuesday	1 Wednesday
7am			
8am			
9am			
10am			
11am			
12pm			
1pm			
2pm			
3pm			
4pm			
5pm			
6pm			
7pm			

Transactions

Category	Amount
	$
	$
	$
	$
	$

Transactions

Category	Amount
	$
	$
	$
	$
	$

Transactions

Category	Amount
	$
	$
	$
	$
	$

Transactions

Category	Amount
	$
	$
	$
	$
	$

2 Thursday

3 Friday

4 Saturday

To Do List

- [ ]
- [ ]
- [ ]
- [ ]
- [ ]
- [ ]
- [ ]
- [ ]
- [ ]
- [ ]
- [ ]
- [ ]
- [ ]
- [ ]
- [ ]
- [ ]
- [ ]
- [ ]
- [ ]
- [ ]
- [ ]
- [ ]
- [ ]
- [ ]
- [ ]
- [ ]
- [ ]
- [ ]
- [ ]
- [ ]
- [ ]
- [ ]
- [ ]
- [ ]

Transactions

Category	Amount
	$
	$
	$
	$
	$

Transactions

Category	Amount
	$
	$
	$
	$
	$

Transactions

Category	Amount
	$
	$
	$
	$
	$

November

November's Budget

Income	Projected	Actual
Total Income		

Savings & Investments	Projected	Actual
Total Savings & Investments		

Expenses	Projected	Actual
Total Expenses		

Ending Balance	Projected	Actual
Total Income - Total Savings & Investments - Total Expenses =		

November 1 - 4

29 Sunday	30 Monday	31 Tuesday	1 Wednesday
			7am
			8am
			9am
			10am
			11am
			12pm
			1pm
			2pm
			3pm
			4pm
			5pm
			6pm
			7pm

Transactions

Category	Amount
	$
	$
	$
	$
	$

Transactions

Category	Amount
	$
	$
	$
	$
	$

Transactions

Category	Amount
	$
	$
	$
	$
	$

Transactions

Category	Amount
	$
	$
	$
	$
	$

2 Thursday

3 Friday

4 Saturday

To Do List

- ☐
- ☐
- ☐
- ☐
- ☐
- ☐
- ☐
- ☐
- ☐
- ☐
- ☐
- ☐
- ☐
- ☐
- ☐
- ☐
- ☐
- ☐
- ☐
- ☐
- ☐
- ☐
- ☐
- ☐
- ☐
- ☐
- ☐
- ☐
- ☐
- ☐
- ☐
- ☐
- ☐
- ☐

Transactions

Category	Amount
	$
	$
	$
	$
	$

Transactions

Category	Amount
	$
	$
	$
	$
	$

Transactions

Category	Amount
	$
	$
	$
	$
	$

November 5 - 11

5 Sunday	6 Monday	7 Tuesday	8 Wednesday
7am			
8am			
9am			
10am			
11am			
12pm			
1pm			
2pm			
3pm			
4pm			
5pm			
6pm			
7pm			

Transactions

Category	Amount
	$
	$
	$
	$
	$

Transactions

Category	Amount
	$
	$
	$
	$
	$

Transactions

Category	Amount
	$
	$
	$
	$
	$

Transactions

Category	Amount
	$
	$
	$
	$
	$

9 Thursday

10 Friday

11 Saturday

To Do List

☐
☐
☐
☐
☐
☐
☐
☐
☐
☐
☐
☐
☐
☐
☐
☐
☐
☐
☐
☐
☐
☐
☐
☐
☐
☐
☐
☐
☐
☐
☐
☐
☐
☐

Transactions

Category	Amount
	$
	$
	$
	$
	$

Transactions

Category	Amount
	$
	$
	$
	$
	$

Transactions

Category	Amount
	$
	$
	$
	$
	$

November 12 - 18

12 Sunday	13 Monday	14 Tuesday	15 Wednesday
7am			
8am			
9am			
10am			
11am			
12pm			
1pm			
2pm			
3pm			
4pm			
5pm			
6pm			
7pm			

Transactions

Category	Amount
	$
	$
	$
	$
	$

Transactions

Category	Amount
	$
	$
	$
	$
	$

Transactions

Category	Amount
	$
	$
	$
	$
	$

Transactions

Category	Amount
	$
	$
	$
	$
	$

16 Thursday	17 Friday	18 Saturday	To Do List
			☐
			☐
			☐
			☐
			☐
			☐
			☐
			☐
			☐
			☐
			☐
			☐
			☐
			☐
			☐
			☐
			☐
			☐
			☐
			☐
			☐
			☐
			☐
			☐
			☐
			☐
			☐
			☐
			☐
			☐
			☐
			☐
			☐
			☐

Transactions

Category	Amount
	$
	$
	$
	$
	$

Transactions

Category	Amount
	$
	$
	$
	$
	$

Transactions

Category	Amount
	$
	$
	$
	$
	$

NOVEMBER 19 - 25

19 SUNDAY	20 MONDAY	21 TUESDAY	22 WEDNESDAY
7am			
8am			
9am			
10am			
11am			
12pm			
1pm			
2pm			
3pm			
4pm			
5pm			
6pm			
7pm			

TRANSACTIONS

Category	Amount
	$
	$
	$
	$
	$

TRANSACTIONS

Category	Amount
	$
	$
	$
	$
	$

TRANSACTIONS

Category	Amount
	$
	$
	$
	$
	$

TRANSACTIONS

Category	Amount
	$
	$
	$
	$
	$

23 Thursday

24 Friday

25 Saturday

To Do List

- [ ]
- [ ]
- [ ]
- [ ]
- [ ]
- [ ]
- [ ]
- [ ]
- [ ]
- [ ]
- [ ]
- [ ]
- [ ]
- [ ]
- [ ]
- [ ]
- [ ]
- [ ]
- [ ]
- [ ]
- [ ]
- [ ]
- [ ]
- [ ]
- [ ]
- [ ]
- [ ]
- [ ]
- [ ]
- [ ]
- [ ]
- [ ]
- [ ]
- [ ]

Transactions

Category	Amount
	$
	$
	$
	$
	$

Transactions

Category	Amount
	$
	$
	$
	$
	$

Transactions

Category	Amount
	$
	$
	$
	$
	$

November 26 - 30

26 Sunday	27 Monday	28 Tuesday	29 Wednesday
7am			
8am			
9am			
10am			
11am			
12pm			
1pm			
2pm			
3pm			
4pm			
5pm			
6pm			
7pm			

Transactions

Category	Amount
	$
	$
	$
	$
	$

Transactions

Category	Amount
	$
	$
	$
	$
	$

Transactions

Category	Amount
	$
	$
	$
	$
	$

Transactions

Category	Amount
	$
	$
	$
	$
	$

30 Thursday

1 Friday

2 Saturday

To Do List

- [ ]
- [ ]
- [ ]
- [ ]
- [ ]
- [ ]
- [ ]
- [ ]
- [ ]
- [ ]
- [ ]
- [ ]
- [ ]
- [ ]
- [ ]
- [ ]
- [ ]
- [ ]
- [ ]
- [ ]
- [ ]
- [ ]
- [ ]
- [ ]
- [ ]
- [ ]
- [ ]
- [ ]
- [ ]
- [ ]
- [ ]
- [ ]
- [ ]
- [ ]

Transactions

Category	Amount
	$
	$
	$
	$
	$

Transactions

Category	Amount
	$
	$
	$
	$
	$

Transactions

Category	Amount
	$
	$
	$
	$
	$

DECEBMER

December's Budget

Income	Projected	Actual
Total Income		

Savings & Investments	Projected	Actual
Total Savings & Investments		

Expenses	Projected	Actual
Total Expenses		

Ending Balance	Projected	Actual
Total Income - Total Savings & Investments - Total Expenses =		

December 1 - 2

26 Sunday

27 Monday

28 Tuesday

29 Wednesday

Transactions

Category	Amount
	$
	$
	$
	$
	$

Transactions

Category	Amount
	$
	$
	$
	$
	$

Transactions

Category	Amount
	$
	$
	$
	$
	$

Transactions

Category	Amount
	$
	$
	$
	$
	$

30 Thursday

1 Friday

2 Saturday

To Do List

- ☐
- ☐
- ☐
- ☐
- ☐
- ☐
- ☐
- ☐
- ☐
- ☐
- ☐
- ☐
- ☐
- ☐
- ☐
- ☐
- ☐
- ☐
- ☐
- ☐
- ☐
- ☐
- ☐
- ☐
- ☐
- ☐
- ☐
- ☐
- ☐
- ☐
- ☐
- ☐
- ☐
- ☐

Transactions

Category	Amount
	$
	$
	$
	$
	$

Transactions

Category	Amount
	$
	$
	$
	$
	$

Transactions

Category	Amount
	$
	$
	$
	$
	$

December 3 - 9

3 Sunday	4 Monday	5 Tuesday	6 Wednesday
7am			
8am			
9am			
10am			
11am			
12pm			
1pm			
2pm			
3pm			
4pm			
5pm			
6pm			
7pm			

Transactions

Category	Amount
	$
	$
	$
	$
	$

Transactions

Category	Amount
	$
	$
	$
	$
	$

Transactions

Category	Amount
	$
	$
	$
	$
	$

Transactions

Category	Amount
	$
	$
	$
	$
	$

7 Thursday	8 Friday	9 Saturday	To Do List
			☐
			☐
			☐
			☐
			☐
			☐
			☐
			☐
			☐
			☐
			☐
			☐
			☐
			☐
			☐
			☐
			☐
			☐
			☐
			☐
			☐
			☐
			☐
			☐
			☐
			☐
			☐
			☐
			☐
			☐
			☐
			☐
			☐
			☐

Transactions

Category	Amount
	$
	$
	$
	$
	$

Transactions

Category	Amount
	$
	$
	$
	$
	$

Transactions

Category	Amount
	$
	$
	$
	$
	$

December 10 - 16

10 Sunday	11 Monday	12 Tuesday	13 Wednesday
7am			
8am			
9am			
10am			
11am			
12pm			
1pm			
2pm			
3pm			
4pm			
5pm			
6pm			
7pm			

Transactions

Category	Amount
	$
	$
	$
	$
	$

Transactions

Category	Amount
	$
	$
	$
	$
	$

Transactions

Category	Amount
	$
	$
	$
	$
	$

Transactions

Category	Amount
	$
	$
	$
	$
	$

14 Thursday

15 Friday

16 Saturday

To Do List

☐
☐
☐
☐
☐
☐
☐
☐
☐
☐
☐
☐
☐
☐
☐
☐
☐
☐
☐
☐
☐
☐
☐
☐
☐
☐
☐
☐
☐
☐
☐
☐
☐
☐

Transactions

Category	Amount
	$
	$
	$
	$
	$

Transactions

Category	Amount
	$
	$
	$
	$
	$

Transactions

Category	Amount
	$
	$
	$
	$
	$

December 17 - 23

17 Sunday	18 Monday	19 Tuesday	20 Wednesday
7am			
8am			
9am			
10am			
11am			
12pm			
1pm			
2pm			
3pm			
4pm			
5pm			
6pm			
7pm			

Transactions

Category	Amount
	$
	$
	$
	$
	$

Transactions

Category	Amount
	$
	$
	$
	$
	$

Transactions

Category	Amount
	$
	$
	$
	$
	$

Transactions

Category	Amount
	$
	$
	$
	$
	$

21 Thursday

22 Friday

23 Saturday

To Do List

☐
☐
☐
☐
☐
☐
☐
☐
☐
☐
☐
☐
☐
☐
☐
☐
☐
☐
☐
☐
☐
☐
☐
☐
☐
☐
☐
☐
☐
☐
☐
☐
☐
☐

Transactions

Category	Amount
	$
	$
	$
	$
	$

Transactions

Category	Amount
	$
	$
	$
	$
	$

Transactions

Category	Amount
	$
	$
	$
	$
	$

December 24 - 30

24 Sunday	25 Monday	26 Tuesday	27 Wednesday
7am			
8am			
9am			
10am			
11am			
12pm			
1pm			
2pm			
3pm			
4pm			
5pm			
6pm			
7pm			

Transactions

Category	Amount
	$
	$
	$
	$
	$

Transactions

Category	Amount
	$
	$
	$
	$
	$

Transactions

Category	Amount
	$
	$
	$
	$
	$

Transactions

Category	Amount
	$
	$
	$
	$
	$

28 Thursday

29 Friday

30 Saturday

To Do List

- [ ]
- [ ]
- [ ]
- [ ]
- [ ]
- [ ]
- [ ]
- [ ]
- [ ]
- [ ]
- [ ]
- [ ]
- [ ]
- [ ]
- [ ]
- [ ]
- [ ]
- [ ]
- [ ]
- [ ]
- [ ]
- [ ]
- [ ]
- [ ]
- [ ]
- [ ]
- [ ]
- [ ]
- [ ]
- [ ]
- [ ]
- [ ]
- [ ]
- [ ]

Transactions

Category	Amount
	$
	$
	$
	$
	$

Transactions

Category	Amount
	$
	$
	$
	$
	$

Transactions

Category	Amount
	$
	$
	$
	$
	$

December 31

31 Sunday	1 Monday	2 Tuesday	3 Wednesday
7am			
8am			
9am			
10am			
11am			
12pm			
1pm			
2pm			
3pm			
4pm			
5pm			
6pm			
7pm			

Transactions

Category	Amount
	$
	$
	$
	$
	$

Transactions

Category	Amount
	$
	$
	$
	$
	$

Transactions

Category	Amount
	$
	$
	$
	$
	$

Transactions

Category	Amount
	$
	$
	$
	$
	$

4 Thursday

5 Friday

6 Saturday

To Do List

- ☐
- ☐
- ☐
- ☐
- ☐
- ☐
- ☐
- ☐
- ☐
- ☐
- ☐
- ☐
- ☐
- ☐
- ☐
- ☐
- ☐
- ☐
- ☐
- ☐
- ☐
- ☐
- ☐
- ☐
- ☐
- ☐
- ☐
- ☐
- ☐
- ☐
- ☐
- ☐
- ☐
- ☐

Transactions

Category	Amount
	$
	$
	$
	$
	$

Transactions

Category	Amount
	$
	$
	$
	$
	$

Transactions

Category	Amount
	$
	$
	$
	$
	$

www.pilunapress.com